BRITAIN IN OLD PHOTOGRAPHS

SOUTHWOLD

JOHN MILLER

SUTTON PUBLISHING LIMITED

Sutton Publishing Limited
Phoenix Mill · Thrupp · Stroud
Gloucestershire · GL5 2BU

First published 1999

Copyright © John Miller, 1999

Title page: Walter Hurr, a fisherman.

British Library Cataloguing in Publication Data
A catalogue record for this book is available from the
British Library.

ISBN 0-7509-2245-1

Typeset in 10.5/13.5 Photina.
Typesetting and origination by
Sutton Publishing Limited.
Printed in Great Britain by
Ebenezer Baylis, Worcester.

Enjoying the sunshine on a crowded beach below Gun Hill, 1912. Three bathing machines are
drawn up at the edge of the sea.

CONTENTS

The lighthouse, soaring powerfully above the huddle of little buildings, was lit for the first time one February night in 1889 and displayed a white occulting light over a distance of 17 miles. When this photograph was taken in the early 1920s Stradbroke Road had nine shops, a sub-post office, a garage and a petrol station. Today many of its dwellings are holiday homes, and in the summer there is an acute parking problem.

INTRODUCTION

One hundred years ago a travel journal devoted entirely to Southwold told its readers: 'Southwold in the opening years of the twentieth century and the coronation year of King Edward VII is one of the brightest, prettiest and quaintest little seaside towns in England, and one of the very healthiest and most beneficial sanitary resorts in the whole United Kingdom.' A touch of hyperbole? Perhaps, but it is a fact that when that piece was written Southwold had indeed emerged as a very special holiday resort on the pebbly edge of eastern England, a little town of unrivalled charms.

Travel writers still cannot leave it alone. We are told that Southwold is caught in a time warp. It is a town that time forgot. It is frozen in the aspic of the 1930s. Or 1940s. Or 1950s. (Which decade depends on the age of the writer.) It has seen no technological advance since the shoehorn! It is an instructive detour for anyone who missed the 1950s. Its crimes could be solved by the Famous Five. And so on and so forth.

In *The Best of Southwold*, also published by Sutton, I revived tens of thousands of words written about the town and its people over several centuries. They were all unfailingly nice. Daniel Defoe, for example, visited Southwold in 1713 and wrote a neat and lovely piece about a million swallows perching on the roof of St Edmund's Church and surrounding houses, poised to fly away. (They had gone the next morning.)

In a foreword to the book Michael Palin confessed he was potty about Southwold, and how the place had become an indelible part of his life. And over the last 150 years writers and journalists have descended on Southwold and have – truly without exception – gone away enthusing excitedly about what they saw and felt, and often of Southwold's gastronomic delights and its beer. (Of course they only come in the summer. They know nothing of those winter days when a bitterly cold wind blows all the way from Siberia and fairly cuts one in two, and the world is drab and grey and wet.) But Southwold apparently does them a world of good. They are happier, better people for visiting the place. It was, and is, some kind of an extraordinary geographical Prozac.

This collection of old photographs of Southwold by and large is centred on the town in the 1890s and the Edwardian days. Ah, those were the days, weren't they? The sun shone from a cloudless sky: we are officially told that in eight months from March to October in 1907 there were only eleven days without sunshine!

Indeed this was the so-called Edwardian golden age, and Southwold was booming. The unique little train brought middle-class families from London and elsewhere complete with maid and cook to a delightful, genteel holiday resort. They came not for a week or two, but for the season, a month or six weeks. They stayed in hotels like the newly built Grand, or the Marlborough, or the converted Centre Cliff, and in numerous boarding houses that did good business.

And – as they do today – they wrote 'wish you were here' postcards. From 1894 when the Post Office lifted monopolistic restrictions and allowed cards to be sent through the post with a halfpenny adhesive stamp, the postcard became an integral part of the seaside scene. The first decade of the twentieth century was the heyday of the postcard.

Southwold also had a stroke of luck. In 1900 Frederick Jenkins turned up in the town and took over a photographer's shop, 94 High Street. Over the next three decades he became firmly established as 'the' Southwold photographer, but more importantly as the man who traced the events of a changing world, and even a changing – albeit ever so slightly – Southwold, through the medium of picture postcards.

There were other photographers too. Some of the most charming and interesting photographs in this book were taken by men whose names have been long forgotten – Albert Jarvis, who briefly had a shop in Station Road before the turn of the century, Clement Tureen, who was active in the 1880s, and especially James Godfrey Martyn, from 1882 to 1900.

Picture postcard companies also moved in – I have traced more than twenty, many of which have pictures in this book – and there were also a host of small beach photographers who targeted Southwold, and who set up tents or used the sea walls as backgrounds before moving on at the end of the season.

But Jenkins stayed, and stayed, to become five times town mayor, and for twenty-nine years a Justice of the Peace, and to run his photographic business and the town's pioneering radio shop.

The secret of his success was simple. He was a good photographer with a wide range of subject interest, and Southwold was by the sea and with its own special narrow gauge railway, and interesting historical background. All he had to do was to wander about with his camera and his tripod – and he took a regular walk along the beach – until something took his fancy and gave him the chance to press the button on immortality. He snapped it all: the railway, the lighthouse, streets and shops, the pier, firemen, children, fishermen, Scots lassies, beach erosion, Trinity Fairs and lifeboat launches, capturing the essentially conservative nature of Southwold with its timeless vivacity and confidence. What is more, he could buy in bulk ready-sensitised cards printed on the other side with a postal divided back. And so he could capture a local event on his camera and issue the postcards almost instantly, perhaps even that afternoon if there were ready customers about.

Not surprisingly he flourished, and when that Edwardian Indian summer was brought to a devastating end by the First World War and the golden age of the postcard was over, and fashions and attitudes changed, Frederick Jenkins survived.

As do these old photographs of a place that John Betjeman (who may or may not have actually visited Southwold) nevertheless brilliantly caught in his poem 'Beside the Seaside':

> Ah! still the same, the same
> As it was last year and the year before
> But rather more expensive now, of course.

CHAPTER ONE
THE BEACH

The coming of the railway brought summer visitors and turned Southwold into a genteel seaside resort. By 1907 the Grand Hotel, with 100 rooms and occupying a prominent seafront site, was firmly established and flourishing. On the beach below it a small typically overdressed crowd has gathered, posing with a boy clinging on to a fish.

The official Southwold Visitors List of 1907 underlined the excellent seabathing and the number of 'first-rate bathing machines' at the north end of the seafront. These were owned by Smith and Palmer and were moved – such as the one at the end of the row in this photograph – by 'Kinie' Palmer who did the pushing, and 'Fie' Smith who operated the winches, known as 'crabs', near the promenade. This was a popular beach with an area set aside for children.

St James Green, 1908. Holidaymakers stroll along the middle of the broad road leading to North Parade and the pier. The town's eight coastguards did their cutlass and flag signalling drill daily in front of the white single-storey Guardship which is now a private dwelling. The buildings to the left have been demolished and completely reconstructed. There is a small boat at the top of the score on the right much used by fishermen. This area was called Cuddy Corner by local people.

A cool and elegant terrace, Centre Cliff was built in about 1830. It became the Centre Cliff Hotel in 1887, and the towering north wing was later reduced to its present two storeys. The flag is flying above the fishermen's lookout post on the lower promenade to the right.

An east wind is blowing strongly off the sea and they are hanging on to their hats for dear life as they stroll along Centre Cliff in 1898. The pier has yet to be built and the wooden v-shaped groynes, which offered some shelter from the wind, have not yet been smashed to pieces by the sea.

A packed Gun Hill beach, 1908. This photograph was turned into a postcard and sent by Tim to a Miss Eveley in Worthing. He drew attention to himself with a cross.

The Jenkins family spending a day on Southwold beach below East Cliff, August 1906. Mrs Maud Jenkins and the nursemaid are sitting with little Barrett, Marjorie and Blyford while Father takes the photograph. Barrett was three times Mayor of Southwold.

Another family relaxing on the beach, 3 July 1925. Despite the way grandmother is dressed, fashions have changed. The huge ladies' hats have been replaced by the cloche, and short hems have arrived. The children too are not so overdressed.

'Waiting for Orders' became a popular postcard in the early 1900s. This one was sent to a Miss Hannah Clipperton of Claygate, Surrey, with much love from 'M' as a postcard of the Grand Hotel where he was staying. He added: 'We are having lovely weather and I am enjoying Southwold very much. I have been out for two sails already and we swim every morning.'

The Children's Special Service Mission has been coming to Southwold every summer since 1901. Many a romance developed from the meetings on the beach so that the letters CSSM came to stand for 'Come Single Soon Married'.

Sandcastles (almost instinctive to children), sea and sunshine at Southwold, August 1907. But perhaps the billowing skirt of the lady with the hat by the seashore indicates the wind is blowing. Writing on this postcard sent to Miss Stone of Great Missenden, Bucks, Stewart comments: 'It is simply glorious weather here and the heat is overpowering. I have had some lovely sea bathing and got quite brown.'

North Parade, 1890. The row of three-storey houses has just been completed, and most of them
offered accommodation to holidaymakers. The 'house to let' sign refers to another newly built

three-storey building. Along the beach is a jumble of fishermen's huts and parts of other buildings in which families had recently lived.

There were bathing machines at the Gun Hill end of the promenade, and for another few years after this picture was taken in 1920. These were run by Sam May. The bathing machine is believed to have been introduced in about 1750 and three were in use on Southwold's beaches in the 1830s.

A boy looks from the window of one of Sam May's high-wheeled bathing machines, 1910. Like insects on wheels they crept down the beach as the tide receded. The last few bathing machines were in use in the early 1930s. They performed one last role: they were dotted about the Common during the Second World War as obstacles to prevent German aircraft from landing. None tried it.

South Beach, 1913. Bathing machines are jumbled together with fishermen's boats and there is a diving raft out to sea. This postcard dated August 1913 reads: 'Having a lovely time. Had my first dip this morning. Thought about you last Sunday. So sorry I shall not be at choir practice this Friday. Love Else P.'

Stanley Aldrich's hut at South Beach sold not only tea and cakes but also buckets and spades and flags for sandcastles. Over the last 150 years Southwold Town Council has fought hard to prevent any vulgarisation of the resort, and has successfully opposed attempts to over-commercialise the seafront.

Sam May was one of the town's most famous characters and readily posed for visitors and local people. Apart from owning bathing machines he was a longshore fisherman and was coxswain of the *Alfred Corry* from 1898 until 1913. Whatever the weather he never failed to get the lifeboat launched. Here he is standing outside his hut on South Beach in 1909 with Mrs Nellie Jarvis, who lived in a grand house in Lorne Road. Sam himself lived in Park Lane, now one of Southwold's most fashionable streets. When his wife died he kept her ashes in the bedroom, but every morning he took them downstairs for breakfast and put them on the kitchen table opposite him.

A view from Gun Hill along the length of California Sands to the lifeboat shed near the harbour, 1894. Hard by the promenade is a popular attraction, the camera obscura: a prism in the roof reflected a panoramic view of the coastline on to a table in the darkened interior. Owned by Ben Lowsey, it was later moved to Centre Cliff.

North Beach was another lively area for both holidaymakers and fishermen. With the building of the pier in 1900 other attractions were provided such as tennis courts and a pond for model yachts. But the sea was to wreak havoc along this stretch of coastline and major concrete defences had to be built.

In the 1890s model yacht regattas took place on a pond in Ferry Road opposite the California Sands. They shifted to the new pond by the pier where there was a charge of 1*d* a go. At the regatta here on 10 August 1907 there were prizes of silver-plated teaspoons in various shapes.

The goatcarts pulled their small passengers from the pier up North Parade to Trinity Street. The sender of this postcard to a Miss Crump of Ashford wrote in July 1914: 'My holiday is going all too quickly. This is a jolly little place but there are too many visitors and many more are expected next month. Baby Margaret enjoys playing in the sand and we have lots of games together. Much love, yours ever D.'

Harbour Road at the height of summer, 1930. The holiday season is in full swing. Motor cars could find a place to
park in those days. You could camp on the beach. There was swimming, horse-riding, boating, and a good walk
along what is now Ferry Road to the harbour where a camp has been set up. Some of the bungalows on the right
were swept away by the floods of 1953. The photograph below of South Beach was taken the same year. The
12 × 8 ft wooden beach hut, a mark of minor privilege in what was already recognised as the mecca of East
Anglia, had arrived.

Gun Hill from California Sands, 1902. The photograph also captures the three Southwold

landmarks of the time, the pier, the lighthouse and St Edmund's Church.

A large crowd gathered on the beach on 21 August 1905 to mark the CSSM's Missions Day. The photograph became this postcard on the following day and was sent to Miss E. Kernon, of the Saracen Head Hotel, Chelmsford, with a cryptic message: 'Find skinny spinster.'

Southwold Baywatch. Before the Second World War the beaches were patrolled by members of a twenty-strong squad of lifeguards of both sexes. Hundreds watched this annual display in 1936 below Kilcock Cliff.

CHAPTER TWO

THE COMMON

The Common is truly Southwold's wonder. Covering some 130 acres it is bounded by marshes and three roads, and almost forms a triangle. You walk, or picnic or play on The Common – as did five children with the 64-pounder cannon in 1910 before it was melted down for scrap. You can play cricket and football and rugby and golf, or listen to the skylarks or watch heron on the marshes or exercise your dog (ensuring of course you observe the law!), or stroll across The Common on your way to the harbour or further afield to Walberswick. It is a very special place of grass, yellow gorse and the odd patch of heather, and it is a delight.

The Common was a place for sport and from 1902 until the early 1920s an annual sports event was held. Apart from the usual races there was a marathon from Lowestoft to Southwold, 2 and 3 mile motorcycle races, and in 1913 The Common witnessed the first landing there of an aeroplane.

The finish of the mile race on The Common, 1908. On the back of a postcard of the finish is written: 'Dear Charles, I hope that is not you in front. Jack is much better at this sort of thing.'

A remarkably lovely windmill, Black Mill, was built in 1798 and for a time was one of three mills in the town. It changed hands several times and suffered from gales and fires before being dismantled in 1894. The St Barnabas home and a house now occupy the site.

Southwold's new water tower was built in 1937 – and it was only a question of time before someone took the first panoramic view of that part of The Common which is now a football pitch, and the town beyond.

This postcard of cows on The Common in 1923 was sent to a Tottenham address. It read: 'We are all enjoying ourselves only the weather is rotten. We all managed to bathe this morning. It was terribly rough but it was lovely. Nonie.'

The cow, photographed in 1896, is from Holmleigh Farm which bordered The Common.

On Friday 19 August 1904 a cricket match was played on The Common between Ladies and Gentlemen. The teams posed together for a photograph that duly became a postcard, which Harry sent to his mother, Mrs C. Ife of Acton House, Southwold, a week later. What we do not know is who won. But we surely can guess.

York Road from The Common, *c.* 1890. Cattle would be driven from various farms in the town to pasture on The Common. York Road was to become a key road linking the town with the harbour.

Southwold Golf Club dates from 1884. It began as a nine-hole course on The Common by permission of the Southwold Corporation. Many local lads such as 'Pony' Moore worked as caddies

as this 1902 photograph shows. Other later caddies Stanley Quantrill and Lennie Doy went on to win the club's major trophies, and to become club captains.

James Braid, a famous professional golfer of the day, was consulted about the course on several occasions and played an exhibition round on 13 September 1898 with Walter Aveston of Cromer. He was invited to play again in 1906 but was told not to come when he asked for a fee of 8 guineas.

In the shadow of the 1886 water tower, Mr A.R. Grubbe is putting out on the fourth hole, appropriately called 'The Tower'. Honorary treasurer for some thirty years, he is wearing a green club coat. It is not known if he sunk his putt.

From the formation of the Southwold Golf Club the ladies had equal privileges with the men, as long as they did not want to play on Sundays. These ladies are playing the seventh hole, 'The Punchbowl'. The first ladies' competition for a prize was held in 1899.

On 9 May 1913 a 60 hp Deperdussin monoplane flew over Southwold to much excitement and landed on The Common. It was piloted by Mr A.G. Miller who showed off the aeroplane at the Whit Monday sports. A piece of the propeller broke off and is displayed in the Town Hall.

The driver of this car which stopped on The Common on 9 June 1918 was Alice Hess. She was photographed by Frederick Jenkins and sent this postcard to her friend in Hillingdon, Middlesex. She wrote: 'I was delighted to get your letter. I am sending you a postcard of my little car and you will see Teddy sitting beside me. This was only taken four days ago, with much love Alice.'

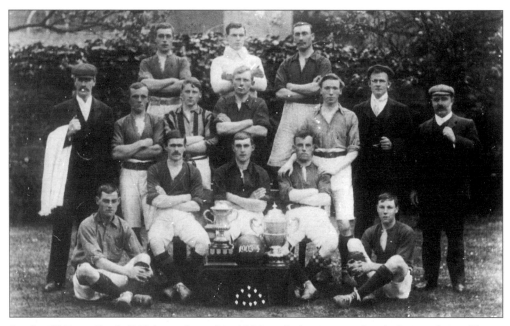

Southwold Town Football Club was formed in 1898, and after it merged with the Beach Ramblers it became a formidable local team. It won the Suffolk Junior Cup final against Trinity Old Boys of Ipswich in 1904, and the side is seen here. Back row, left to right: W. Howard, E. Gill (Captain), C. Goldsmith. Middle row: Duke Osborne (trainer – who is smoking!), Jack May, W. Waller, M. Goldsmith, Jim Jillings, Ted Bailey, C. Fowler. Front row: D. Ladd, F. Reeve, C. Howard, J. Hurren and Binks Palmer.

A mixed doubles tennis match on The Common, 1894. Predictably, for those days, the ladies are wearing long petticoats and flowing skirts with bustles at the back, suggesting the match surely was played at a much more leisurely pace than nowadays.

Two small boys stand at a gateway on to The Common. They are André Jarvis, aged four, and his brother John, aged five, who was mayor of Southwold in 1963. Lt Col. John Jarvis lived in The Elms in Lorne Road, and when he moved into a new house further along the road he took the name with him. He said he had some new headed notepaper printed which he did not want to waste.

Every year between 1931 and 1938 a remarkable experiment aimed at mixing the social classes was carried out on The Common for the week of August Bank Holiday. At the Duke of York's Camp some four hundred boys drawn from public schools and the working class were brought together, living in tents, playing games on The Common and swimming in the sea. The Southwold cinema is on the right of the picture.

Rocket firing practice was regularly carried out on The Common by the coastguards in the early 1900s. Here they are assembling rescue equipment watched by three curious onlookers, including a lad with a very large flat hat.

CHAPTER THREE

PEOPLE

*Southwold's first council houses were opened in
1905 and the King family were the first occupants
of 15 St Edmund's Road. To mark the occasion
Mr King gathered his family around him in the
back garden. He is holding Agnes; her sisters are
Ida and Cissie. Mrs King has her arm around little
Tommy, who is wearing his sailor suit.*

This splendid school photograph was taken in May 1911, as shown by the message on the blackboard being held by one of the boys. Almost certainly there was no school uniform for these sons of Southwold's fishermen and labourers, but they are all wearing sturdy boots to keep their feet dry.

The Southwold School senior class of 1927. Back row, left to right: Sidney Rogers, Fred Manning, Warren Harrison, Stanley Quantrill, Edward Waters, Pryse King. Third row: Tommy Fletcher, Percy Waters, Victor Warby, Tommy Doy, Victor Watson, Frank Kent, Bobby Fryett, Jimmy Stannard, George Deal, Jimmy Smith. Second row: Joan Cross, ? Barnes, Phyllis Ladd, Lily Webb, ? Read, Gwen Brown, Betty Mayhew, Esme May, Ruby May, Rene Stannard, Dorothy Stannard. Front row: Peggy Mullender, Trixie James, Joan Oakley, Phyllis Palmer.

The Southwold School Band of 1935. Two members of the band were identical twins, the May brothers, grandsons of the legendary lifeboat coxswain Sam May.

Eversley Preparatory School opened on The Common in 1895. The school's headmaster in this photograph is Alan Bottomley, who taught at the school for forty years and was headmaster for nearly twenty-five. He retired in 1994, and the school was closed four years later. (Stephen Wolfenden)

They wore their best hats for festivities in the Market Square to mark the coronation of George V on 23 June 1911. The twin girls in the front row on the left of the photograph are identically dressed complete with large round hats.

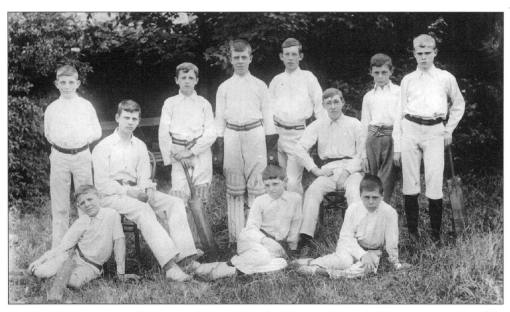

The Eversley School cricket team of 1910 played its matches on The Common against other preparatory school sides in Norfolk and Suffolk, and with mixed fortunes. Between 1902 and 1914 the 1st XI played seventy-nine matches, winning thirty-two. One of Eversley's most famous old boys was G.E. Collins, who introduced gliding to Britain. He was the first pilot to fly a glider some distance upside down, but was killed falling from his plane at 2,000 ft in 1935.

Two teachers from St Felix prepare themselves for a dip in the sea from a bathing machine in the summer of 1909. One teacher is showing the accepted inch or two of knee below her gathered knickers.

The St Felix School photograph of 1900, taken in the garden of May Place. The school started up in
Aldeburgh in 1897 with just seven pupils but within a year had moved to Southwold, establishing

close links with the town which survived the move to Reydon.

The town's roadsweeper during the early Edwardian years was Jimmer Howard, shown here with his daughter in the Market Square. He was so delighted with the Southwold Corporation giving him a new barrow that he wheeled his daughter around the town in it to celebrate. Nearly a hundred years later his successor, Johnny Graham, won a national 'Silver Broom' award for keeping the town's streets clean.

The Sole Bay Brewery, run by a Mr Ernest Adnams, was brewing some five thousand barrels a year when this photograph was taken in 1895. The employees and their families are off to Great Yarmouth for their annual holiday.

The Girls Friendly Society was founded by women to help poor working-class girls find work. For some reason it thrived in Southwold, and this photograph was taken at Wangford on 11 July 1922. In this photograph are Lilly Self, Violet Stannard, Ellen Watson, Celia Stone, Cissie Goldsmith, Fanny Fall, Mrs Tooke, Hilda Tooke, Minnie Green, Nena Ludbroke, Nurse Hughes, Mrs Manning, Leona Watson, Miss Boyden, Amy Ralph, A. Chandler and Mrs Boyden.

St Barnabas, a holiday home for impoverished working ladies, was opened in Southwold to mark Queen Victoria's Jubilee in 1897. Its founder was Miss Mary Shipley, a writer of helpful religious guides, who is seen here sitting in her quaint Edwardian study in 1903.

The 1st Southwold Boy Scout troop was registered on 16 August 1909 and was originally a so-called 'holiday troop'. It was raised by Leonard Spiller, a young vicar who had started troops in London and Cambridge, from boys who were spending their summer holidays in Southwold and were at ease with local lads. The emphasis was on seamanship.

In the Edwardian days coal was king, and Southwold could not have survived without it. The coal merchant of the day was Mr Foulchard of Lorne Road, who delivered by horse and cart from his depot in Spinners Lane.

Southwold Boy Scouts were a lively bunch in 1948. Formed into four patrols they camped on The Common, had camp fire singsongs which would go on well into the night, and even had night exercises. The scoutmaster was Lance May, and among the scouts are John Winter, twice mayor of Southwold, Denis Stannard, John Purdy, John Goldsmith, Peter Crick, David Stannard, David Winter, B. Rivett, R. Palmer, L. Hambling, K. Farrington, P. Townsend, and D. Jessop.

Mr John Seaman married Miss Clara May in the Methodist church on East Green in the summer of 1912. The occasion was a good excuse for the ladies to get out their huge hats embellished with flowers, feathers and satin, and this photograph was taken at the reception, held in the back garden of a house on South Green.

The 1st Company Baden-Powell Girl Guides was formed in June 1910 and consisted of three officers including the captain Miss Mary Holmes, two patrol leaders and twelve guides. By 1921 when this photograph was taken it was thriving, with forty guiders and guides and twelve brownies.

The Jenkins family lived over the shop at 94 High Street. Apart from running a photographic business Frederick Jenkins also sold early wirelesses, components and batteries. In this photograph his children, Peggy, Marjorie and Howard, are managing to both read their books and listen through headphones to their new wireless, a two-valve 1923 Marconiphone.

Holding hands, two small children pose for their photograph at Fazey's Quay after the new harbour was completed in 1907.

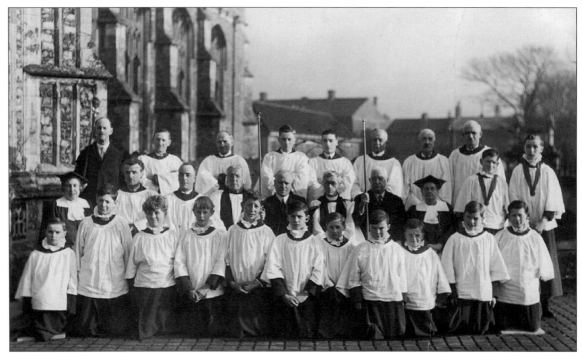

St Edmund's Church choir, January 1940, when the vicar was the Rev. Ronald Pyke, the choirmaster Mr H. Palfrey, and the organist Mr Freddy Neal. The choir was considerably reduced in numbers in the summer of that year when the local school was evacuated.

Fire has scarred the face of Southwold over the centuries: the church was destroyed in 1430 and little of the town survived the 1659 fire. The Fire Service was established in 1883 and the brigade of the late 1920s is pictured here. Back row, left to right: Rush, Hare, Belcher, Chapman, Fulcher, J. Alan, Harvey, Moyes, Thompson. Front row: Bennett, James, Alan, Hurr, and Goodman.

One of the worst fires between the wars destroyed Denny's General Store and a house in the High Street in April 1930. Another store was built on the site.

The retained firemen and their fire engine have operated from several sites since 1890 including the Town Hall, Trinity Street, and Station Road. Since 1964 their home has been on a site near the police station. At the opening of the new station the brigade was twelve-strong. Back row, left to right: Carol Kett, Gordon Julings, John Enby and Joe Jessop. Front row: Tony Sutton, Tom Davies, Sheppy Smith, Leslie Barber, Sam Cooper, Philip Palmer and Dick Wright.

The Southwold Red Cross detachment was formed in 1910. This lovely picture was taken of three of its founder members, the Jellicoe sisters, Kathleen, Mabel and Hilda, in 1912. Mabel's devoted service to the Red Cross in the town for some sixty years and her involvement in other organisations was rewarded with a British Empire Medal in 1962.

When the First World War broke out the Red Cross in Southwold was up and running. Its commandant was Mrs Kathleen Mullock, wife of the local doctor, and the detachment included Miss Constance Grubbe, Nurse Hughes, Monica Williams, Nurse Dimmock, Mary Debney, Mary Holmes, Ethel Holmes and Kathleen Debney.

Frederick Jenkins took this photograph of the local Red Cross detachment in August 1914, and quickly brought it out as a popular patriotic postcard.

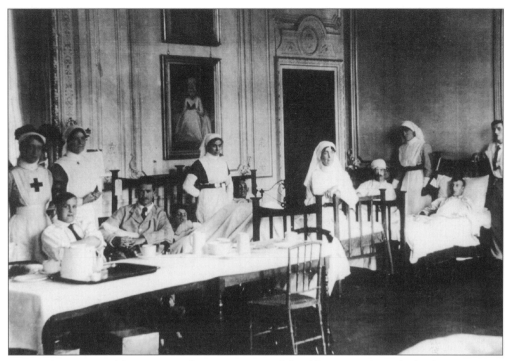

During the First World War more than 1,700 wounded soldiers were brought back from France and taken to Henham Hall, near Southwold, for surgery and convalescence. The nursing staff was largely drawn from the Southwold Red Cross, and Dr Mullock was the Medical Officer.

Dr Richard Mullock was a remarkable surgeon who came to Southwold after serving in the Boer War, with the sole aim of working at the new hospital opened in 1903. Southwold mourned when he died in 1928 at the early age of fifty-two. At his funeral shops closed and local people lined the streets. His grave is in St Edmund's churchyard opposite his beloved hospital and as near to it as he could possibly be.

The town stocks were deliberately placed near the church wall so culprits could be seen by those going to services. They were last used in 1850 by a man who stole eggs from a farm. These stocks replaced the original ones and the 'villains' in this 1911 photograph are young André and John Jarvis with their stepfather George Ludovichi. The present stocks date from 1984.

Mrs Beatrice Bailey and her daughter Beattie in the back yard of 17 High Street, 1910. Nailed to the wall over the door is a horseshoe for good luck. Mr Harry Bailey was a fisherman.

The Town Band of 1882 is playing outside the Crown Inn in the High Street. The band was linked to the raising of the Volunteers at the time of the Napoleonic Wars. This is one of the oldest photographs in this collection. The frontage of the Crown is virtually unchanged today.

The 1906 General Election, known as the 'Food Taxes' election, produced a landslide victory for the Liberal Party, and also signalled the emergence of the Labour Party. A Mr Beauchamp won the Southwold seat for the Liberals as his supporters in this photograph had forecast.

Southwold Jack, at the west end of St Edmund's Church, is a brightly coloured wooden figure dating from the fifteenth century. For many years he has struck his bell at the start of each service, and has also welcomed brides on their wedding day. In 1928 he was taken down and freshened up so well by Cliff Aytoe and 'Straw' Upcraft that you can now make out his blood-flecked eyes and five o'clock shadow.

CREW OF "VOORWAARTZ" RESCUED BY SOUTHWOLD LIFEBOAT.

The Dutch schooner *Voorwaartz* went ashore at Minsmere on the night of 17 January 1912 and the Southwold lifeboat the *Alfred Corry* went to her aid in very rough seas. The lifeboat was itself in danger of being swept ashore, but eventually the crew of four men and the captain's wife were taken off and brought to Southwold.

Every now and again the town turns on the full panoply of civic pomp, and one of those who plays a leading role is the smartly uniformed bellman, or town crier – a much coveted job. Before and after the Second World War it was Jack Button, who was wont to finish off his performance with a rousing 'It's So Lovely on the Pier'. Mr Doddington, the first town crier, is depicted in stained glass in the Town Hall.

Crowds would gather to hear the Town Band which was called upon to perform at all civic functions. The personnel of the band of 1908 are Ernie Howard, George Spence, Jim Sagin, Tommy Land, Tom Blowers, Ted Fish, H. Bedingfield, Will Wright and Ted Cox. It was disbanded in 1926, but half a century later the youthful Southwold and Reydon Corps of Drums was formed to wide acclaim.

Billy Blowers was one of several blacksmiths in the town but was considered to be enough of a character to warrant his picture and autograph on a postcard on sale in 1907.

CHAPTER FOUR

THE SEA

The sea has given a living to hundreds of Southwold fishermen, boat builders, and wreck salvagemen over the years and has been one of the chief reasons why the town has become a much-loved holiday resort. But the sea has been cruel, on the attack, constantly and remorselessly. This photograph of a boy at the sea edge looking at the wreck of the SS Hawk was taken at low tide, at 5.30 p.m. on 22 September 1892. The steamer foundered off Southwold beach on 20 November 1862.

For hundreds of years the coast around Southwold has been eroding. The town has fought back with wooden v-shaped groynes at the bottom of the cliffs, but lacked financial backing to tackle the problem seriously. The floods of January 1905 shook the Corporation as well as residents, who flocked to Gun Hill to see the extent of the flooding.

In effect the January 1905 floods turned Southwold into an island, cutting it off from neighbouring Reydon. This photograph was taken from the entrance to the town with Reydon in the distance.

March 1906 saw more punishment from the sea. York Cliff was severely damaged, leaving two houses overhanging the beach. The scene was turned into a sombre postcard from a Mr and Mrs Grindell to their children in Norwich: 'What the end will be cannot be known but we must leave it to Him who ruleth all things, and He alone can stop it. But there is nothing but destruction to look at from the centre cliff.'

Gun Hill and South Beach were also ravaged by the 1906 floods, and the many fishermen who had their sheds and boats on California Sands must have known that it was only a question of time before they had to move. A postcard sent to Halifax from DW commented: 'This will remind you what the sea has been doing lately to this lovely place.'

The floods in February 1907 were also turned into postcards. But this one is an oddity. It cannot be genuine, and may well have been tampered with. The £2,000 an acre sign surely gives the game away.

The Gun Hill beach was again seriously eroded by the high tides and rough seas of 1907. The Casino, or Roundhouse as it came to be known, was not threatened then, or later.

The seas of February 1938 were particularly rough with 50-ft waves crashing against the modest sea defences, and destroying almost all of the 100 beach huts along the lower promenade, with a great many of them being swept out to sea. The future for the beach hut did not look good. In fact as recently as 1998, and in the space of two hours, 10 of the 140 huts were reduced to matchwood and 47 badly damaged.

Hurricane-force winds combined with high tides in February 1953 swamped the sea defences along the country's east coast from Lincolnshire to Kent, drowning at least 280 people. A great wall of water struck Southwold at both the north and south end of the town. Five died when a dozen homes were swept away in Ferry Road, as shown in this photograph.

During the devastating onrush of the North Sea in 1953 the inside of the pier's amusement arcade was reduced to shambles. Waves and shingle poured in, destroying the bar and pushing over the games machines like ninepins. The good news was that the new reinforced concrete sea wall built in front of much of the town after the Second World War and topped by a promenade all the way from 100 yards north of the pier to Gun Hill withstood the seas.

In 1926 a new motor lifeboat arrived in Southwold. It was the 46-ft *Mary Scot*, named after a woman who had devoted her life to charity. Now Southwold lifeboatmen had both sail and motor power, and the naming and launch of the lifeboat at the harbour drew a huge crowd. In 1940 the *Mary Scot* was handed over to the Royal Navy and was used in the extraordinary evacuation of Dunkirk. Somehow she got back to Dover and finished her time on reserve stations before retiring in 1951.

Opposite: The sea claimed another victim when the beautiful, defiant, and still dignified old barque, the *Idun*, ran aground on Southwold beach on 17 January 1912. The crew were saved by breeches buoy while local salvage hunters surrounded her waiting to move in for the kill.

Lifeboat Day in Southwold was traditionally held over the August Bank Holiday and was a major attraction. The lifeboat, in 1906 the *Alfred Corry*, was paraded through the town preceded by the Town Band and often drawn by Adnams dray horses. After being condemned in 1918 the lifeboat later had a remarkable reprieve. It became a houseboat but her final resting place is back in Southwold, in the former Cromer lifeboat shed repositioned at the harbour in 1998.

The 44-ft Norfolk and Suffolk lifeboat the *Alfred Corry* carried a crew of eighteen hands and had twelve oars. It was Southwold's third lifeboat, in use from 1893 to 1918, and was credited with saving some fifty lives. This launching took place in 1902.

The first lifeboat shed was below the Coastguard Station on St James Green. This was washed away in 1862. A new shed was built on California Sands and was in use until 1925, when the *Mary Scot* arrived and was moored in the harbour while a new shed was built near the ferry slip. The lifeboatmen were photographed in 1931. Back row, left to right: Joe Palmer, 'Popeye' Palmer, 'Bludgeon' Palmer, 'Worky' Upcraft, Johnny Critten, K. Albany. Middle row: B. Stannard, Albert Stannard, Crissy Stannard, Erno May, Jack Palmer, John Wells. Front row: Jack Herrington, 'Slummy' Ashmenall, Frank Upcraft, the coxswain, Mrs Horsfall of Dunwich, Fred Mayhew, and Mr Ernest Read Cooper, the secretary.

Southwold sought to take advantage of the boom in North Sea herring fishing congestion at
Lowestoft and Yarmouth by building a good harbour to replace the one that had become derelict by
1890. Fasey, a London firm, got the contract to widen the entrance and build a quay 1,000 ft long,
a roadway and pickling plots.

The first pile at the harbour was driven by the Countess of Stradbroke in August 1907. Also at the
ceremony were the Mayor, Dr D.H. Howard Tripp, the Town Clerk Mr E.R. Cooper, the Macebearer
and the Vicar.

Southwold beach, 1895. In those days the shore above high water mark was lined with numerous blacktarred and tiled fishermen's huts for storing nets and gear. Their boats would be hauled up by a prehistoric form of capstan. Some 300 men and boys were making a living from fishing.

A punt gliding along the seashore, *c.* 1905. More than forty boats worked off the beach which was divided into family groups, the beach companies, who were fiercely competitive. Twenty years later the number of sailing punts trawling off the coast for herrings, sprats, shrimps, sole, cod and mackerel had doubled, but this was the heyday. The fishing grounds within reach of the punts could not support all these boats, and thereafter the fleet declined in number.

The town seen from the sea, 1901. The huts and the fishing boats below the promenade were soon to

be swept away by rough seas and gales. Many of the buildings above the promenade are unchanged.

The first Scottish herring fleet drifter entered the new harbour on 25 October 1907 and there was a big crowd to welcome it. It was followed by dozens of others and in the following year nearly 300 drifters arrived. In 1909 there were 761 but Southwold was not popular with the North Sea fleet, and the weather and a poor season meant that after 1912 few drifters came.

Two Southwold ladies have pushed the perambulator all the way to the harbour, where they posed for a photograph in 1909. Several steam drifters are tied up and smoke is coming from one of the 'woodbine' funnels, so called because of their resemblance to a popular cheap cigarette of the time. Barrels of herring are lined up and ready for loading on to steamships which will take them to Germany and the Baltic States, which particularly liked the 'Scotch cure'. More than 7,000 crans of the 'silver darlings' were landed in 1909, and 350,000 mackerel.

Opposite: Large numbers of Scottish fishergirls came to Edwardian Southwold by special trains. Many lodged in Walberswick and were rowed to work across the River Blyth. Working in teams of three they gutted the herring at great speed with razor-sharp knives, and packed them in barrels filled with brine. Other lassies worked in the smokehouses producing kippers and bloaters.

The fish market at the harbour was known locally as the Kipperdrome. The Scottish boats and curers came in some strength in 1911 but after that fewer and fewer appeared. The First World War effectively killed off the fish market as a successful and profitable concern. Local youths used it for roller skating, and when it was dismantled wooden sheds sprung up along Ferry Road and elsewhere in Southwold. The area became a caravan park, and all that remains of the fish market is the central wall in the public toilets at the entrance.

Fishermen's huts below the centre of North Parade, 1902. In the summer the longshore fishermen spent their time trawling or shrimping all day long but they still had to repair their nets. Unusually one of the men is wearing a bowler hat. At the bottom of the score is a woman pushing a pram. A concrete promenade was built over the shingle path long ago, and some 230 beach huts, often quaintly named and brightly painted, have replaced the sheds.

The beach below Gun Hill, 1902. This part of Southwold history can only be recaptured by the
photograph: longshore fishermen working on their nets, a solitary high-wheeled bathing machine,

and the pier, most of which some fifty years on had disappeared into the sea.

Southwold fishermen relied on a good sprat harvest between August and November to provide them with a living.
This photograph, with the pier pavilion in the background, was taken in 1925, a good year, when the sprats sold
at 6*d* a bushel. The sprats are being shaken out of the *Cragie's* nets. Traditionally sprats were always on the menu
at the mayor's annual lunch, in those days in November. During the Second World War the sprat season dropped
away and never recovered.

CHAPTER FIVE

THE TOWN

The arrival of the incredible performing Russian bear and his gypsy handler by horse and cart – imagine the commotion – was guaranteed to bring out the children in Southwold in the early 1900s. This was street theatre, and there were no concerns about traffic. Nor come to that of political correctness: the bear was chained to a wall in the garden of a doss house off the High Street. In the background is Barclays Bank which took over the site in 1897, and still occupies it a hundred years later.

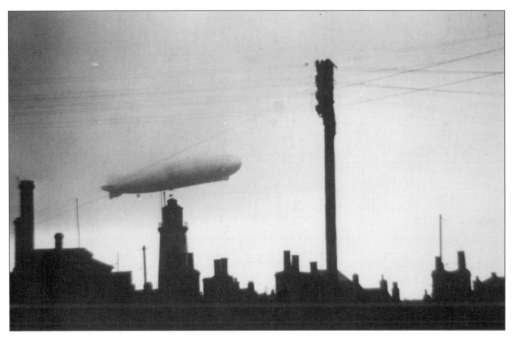

This remarkable photograph of the German airship the Graf Zeppelin passing over the lighthouse was taken at 2.47 in the afternoon on 19 August 1931. The airship had taken off from Hanworth Aerodrome near Wembley and flown round Britain in a clockwise direction. It was flying unusually low because of the bad weather and low cloudbase. Some elderly Southwold inhabitants were unhappy about the flight as the town had been the target of a Zeppelin raid in the First World War.

The town was visited by a civil Short Empire flying boat, the *Caledonia*, in 1936. Nowadays military aircraft regularly fly over Southwold at low altitudes.

The lighthouse was completed in 1890 and it was only a question of time before somebody realised there was a good picture to be taken from the top of it. This was one photograph of a set of six possibly taken by Donald Gooding, who put together a collection of valuable documents, maps and photographs about the town. The area north of the lighthouse changed dramatically in the next few years after the East Coast Development Company had bought the Town Farm from the Corporation. Note the washing hanging out on a line in the back garden of a house in Chester Road.

The Market Square, 1886. The tiny triangular market-place has the dimensions of a film set and
the postures of the men and the way they are stretched out across the road suggest it could be a

western. Looking towards East Street the Town Hall and the Swan are on the left. Moore was the post office, grocer and draper, and the last building in the row was formerly the town gaol.

South Green, 1905. Flags are flying so it must have been a special occasion. This postcard was sent on 24 December to a Mrs Wright in London from a Mrs Wales who wrote: 'Just a line to thank you for your kind Christmas present.'

The Market Place, 1900. Until 1809 there was an ancient market cross. The pump was presented to the town in 1873 with its town crest of frolicking herrings and motto 'Defend they Ryght'. It was a water standby during the Second World War but is no longer operating.

These four humble cottages fronted Barnaby Green and may have been among the few dwellings to have survived the fire of 1659. One of them was occupied by William Briggs, a cowkeeper, and another by John Hammond, who let out rooms. In 1914 they were replaced by a solid two-storey Edwardian house, and a shop.

Chester Road, 1909. A couple of houses in this road have a lighthouse almost literally in their back garden. This was a postcard sent to Hautbois Old Hall, Coltishall, Norwich, with the comment: 'I send you our hen coup basking in the sunshine. Keep this as I want it. Have you blown up any rabbits yet? MN.'

St Edmund's Church from Hollyhock Square, early 1900s. On 15 May 1943 German aircraft dropped four bombs near the church. A direct hit on the houses of Hollyhock Square on the left of the photograph killed seven people. The explosions destroyed the Victorian glass in every window of the church except that of the great west end.

One of the town's most attractive small buildings, the Museum dates from the second half of the seventeenth century. It was a weaver's cottage until it was converted into a museum in 1933, when this photograph was taken.

Gun Hill is the town's most prominent feature, an open grass plot between some fine houses and the sea. Its six cannon were issued for coastal defence in 1746 and were used for festive occasions until a tragic event in 1850 when one failed to fire, and a volunteer gunner looked down the barrel to see what had happened.

Gun Hill, 1902. The St Felix schoolgirls sitting on the seat appear to have decided they were not going to be photographed and have covered their faces with their straw hats and parasols. The seats are now placed facing the sea. Southwold Town Council is responsible for more than 200 seats named for people who loved the town.

Salt was panned for several hundred years at a creek near what is now the start of Ferry Road. Competition slowly destroyed the salt works, but there was a thriving hot salt bathhouse built to cash in on the early Victorian craze of taking sea waters for health reasons. The brine was pumped by the windmill along troughs to the bathhouse where it was heated by coal. The salt works and the baths closed in the early 1890s.

North Parade, 1908. Amid great excitement Fossett's Circus has arrived for a summer season and is parading around the town to get some publicity. On the left of this superb animated picture there is an elephant, and the backsides of two camels can be seen near the street lamp.

St Barnabas, 1910. Facing The Common and with a wonderful view of the sea and over the marshes to Walberswick, this home for impoverished working ladies had great difficulty finding both funds, and visitors in the winter. It was then run by Helen Perry and her friend Ethel Miller, who rode about Southwold in tandem on the double tricycle parked outside the home.

Lorne Road, 1922. Much of this charming road was badly damaged by two 1,000 lb bombs dropped on the town on 21 August 1940. Three houses were demolished. There were only three minor casualties as the town had been partly evacuated. The elegant house on the right now called May Place was built in about 1830.

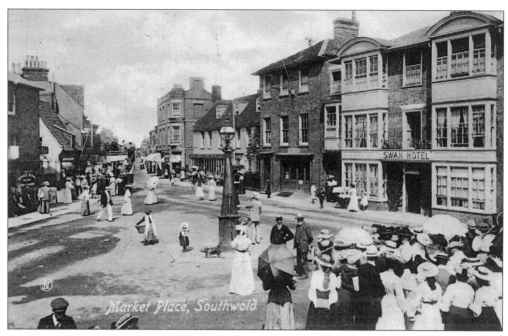

A fashionable crowd has gathered in the Market Place for some unknown occasion in 1912. The postcard was sent from 'M' who was staying in a boarding house in Dunwich Road. She wrote: 'I am sorry to hear Violet has been so poorly and hope she is better, and you too. My mother is looking very well, the sun caught her at once but has hardly touched me at all and I am afraid at present I do no credit to the Southwold air. It is so lovely sitting close by the sea in a comfy hammock chair and with the sun shining brilliantly.'

The High Street, 1926. The last seventy-five years have seen hardly any change in the frontage of buildings on either side of the road. But today the three women with the bicycle would not be able to stroll down the middle of the road.

The row of shops and houses bordering South Green, probably early 1880s. The ladder suggests a roof is being repaired. It is now the site of the Homestead, a private house.

South Green, 1889. The largest of Southwold's many greens, it was where the gentry took root on discovering the benefits of the seaside holiday. Fishermen's cottages were pulled down and replaced with comfortable marine villas. Behind the flagpole in the middle of the photograph is the Red Lion, the oldest survival of the green before the changes.

Another postcard of the top end of the High Street and the Market Square, *c.* 1890. A large dog is standing in the middle of the road.

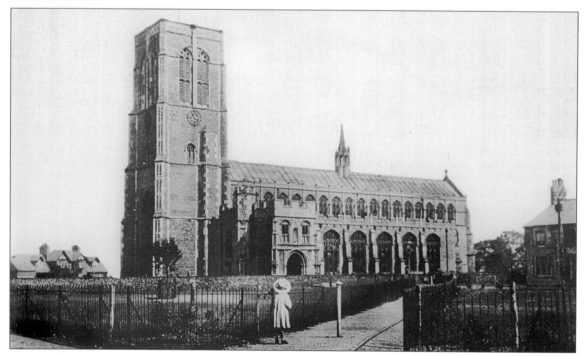

The finest medieval coastal church in England, St Edmund's stands in the centre of the town, and dominates it. The present cathedral-like building was completed in about 1460. The tower stands 100 ft high. This photograph dates from about 1900 – and the small admirer is unknown.

Interior of St Edmund's, autumn 1903: the church marks the harvest of the sea. Fishing nets are hung in swags along the north and south aisles. Fishermen and lifeboatmen brought bundles of rolled-up nets to be laid at the altar. Note the lamps which have been adorned for the occasion, and have since been removed. This photograph was taken from a large glass plate negative, and is published here for the first time.

The High Street, 1910. The first building on the left was the Congregational church. It was opened in 1837 and restored in 1895; in 1972 it became part of the United Reformed church. There are some scaffolding poles at the end of the High Street where work had begun on enlarging the post

office to mark the coronation of George V. There is a row of footscrapers outside the doors of the houses and shops on the right-hand pavement.

An unusual picture of the Sole Bay Brewery from the eastern end of Victoria Street, 1959. On the left side of the street some cottages were being demolished, and later several garden rooms were built for the Swan Hotel.

Billy Blowers, registered shoeing smith and farrier, had his forge at the lower end of Victoria Street, and there was another blacksmith less than 100 yards further up the road. This picture was taken in 1904. The lighthouse can be seen in the distance.

Southwold was first lit by gas in 1848, and half a century later there were forty-five gas street lamps on clockwork time switches. The gas works was situated in Station Road. In 1958 street lamps were converted to electricity and the gas works closed down the following year. The site is now Crick Court, homes for the elderly, and named after George Crick who was manager of the works for forty-two years.

The Southwold Cinema opened in 1912 in the Assembly Rooms in York Road. It advertised itself: 'The best and most up-to-date films are used in this picture palace, and include instruction, humour and tragedy. The Palace is noted for the excellent lighting and steadiness of the pictures.' James Blyth ran the cinema for thirty-eight years and it closed shortly after he retired in 1959. The whole town was sad, but with the arrival of television they stopped going to the cinema. The York Road Surgery was built on the site in 1985.

The first mass was said in the Catholic church on 22 June 1916, the feast of Corpus Christi. The church has a belfry, but no bells. There was a certain amount of opposition to its being built and a condition was imposed before the sale that no bell should ever be rung. Father St Leger-Mason served the town for forty-three years, and when he died in 1940 he was buried in the Catholic part of St Edmund's cemetery.

The School of Industrial Art was opened in Park Lane in 1896. It provided winter time works for some fifty young fishermen, who were its pupils and who were able to add to their incomes with carved chairs, tables, settees and panelling they made when the fishing season was over. One of its most outstanding craftsmen was William Tooke, whose work in silver pewter earned the appreciation of the royal family. He was also responsible for the carved front to the school. It closed in 1914 and is now a private house.

The Grand Hotel, 1954. With the arrival of the railway and the building of the pier, Southwold began to develop its tourism. The Grand Hotel was built to cater for the well-to-do in 1901 at a cost of £30,000. It occupied a prominent seafront site, had 100 rooms, tennis courts, a magnificent lounge, a billiards and smoking room. Its sanitary arrangements were 'as perfect as modern science can make them'. The Second World War did for the Grand Hotel, as it was taken over by the Army and never recovered. Left empty, it was reduced in height for conversion into flats but was totally demolished in 1959. There are modern bungalows on the site, but much of the old garden wall remains.

Methodism was brought to Southwold in 1799 by several Wesleyan preachers. The present chapel on East Green dates from 1835, and the schoolroom, now a popular lecture hall, was built in 1902. Extended in 1919 after this picture was taken, it had a remarkable organist, Mrs Irene Limmer, who held the post for seventy-five years.

The lighthouse, and the lighthouse keeper, at the time of its building, 1890. The railway brought the million and a half tons of bricks for the tower, which stands 120 ft above high water, and the lantern which weighed 8 tons. It was electrified in 1938 with a 1,500 watt lamp, and automated, flashing four times every twenty seconds. In the early 1900s it could be inspected from 9 a.m. until one hour before sunset. Nowadays it is opened to the public once a year.

CHAPTER SIX

WAR & PEACE

Wildly enthusiastic crowds celebrated Queen Victoria's Diamond Jubilee on 22 June 1897. As she went in procession in an open carriage to St Paul's, Southwold marked the occasion with a huge party in the High Street. Tables stretched for 300 yards, and every Southwold person was invited. There were 150 waiters, and 50 carvers of roast beef. Some 500 bread rolls were baked and the meal ended with plum pudding. This party set a pattern for other such occasions in the next century.

The siege, and relief, of Ladysmith, an obscure town in South Africa, was a central military event of the 1899–1902 Boer War. When the news reached London the country exploded into a spontaneous outburst of joy and triumphal celebration, and Southwold joined in. This unique photograph shows the Mayor announcing the news in the Market Square in March 1900. A large number of St Felix girls wearing white straw hats and the odd tam-o-shanter are in the crowd.

Southwold had municipal housing as early as 1905. This photograph is of the opening of sixteen houses in St Edmund's Road by William Thompson, who was born in Southwold and left to become an authority on housing problems. By 1948 about 10 per cent of all houses in the town belonged to the Corporation.

The year 1911 was full of pageantry. On 23 June George V was crowned head of the world's greatest empire and the significance of the event was not lost on loyal patriotic Southwold. The town became a riot of banners and Union flags. The day began with Beating the Bounds, followed by a parade headed by the Town Band from Gun Hill to St Edmund's Church. The sun shone that day, which was fortunate because a feast was held with tables stretching from the Post Office in the High Street to the Market Square. More than a thousand Southwold folk sat down to feast, and there was a bottle of beer for every person, almost certainly a gift from Adnams. Other events included a competition for the best-dressed house, there were mugs for the children, and a procession and a huge bonfire on The Common in the evening. Southwold went home tired but happy.

The First World War started on 4 August 1914 and the Town Clerk wrote in his diary: 'Our visitors almost in a state of panic, our newspaper shops are besieged, spymania has set in and old women in trousers are worrying the authorities.' A month later a meeting was held in front of the Town Hall to recruit men for the new army. Posters put up around the town said: 'Young Men of Southwold and District. Your King and Country need you.'

The war affected Southwold little. The Cycle Company of the Royal Sussex Regiment arrived in August 1914, dug some trenches here and there above the beach and left the following July. Being a town of no military importance, Southwold was not fortified. The message on the back of this postcard said: 'Dear Else. We are having a ripping time here at the seaside just for one week. There are so many things of interest at sea all of which indicate war. It is so dark at nights that we often go astray and then get challenged by sentries. Much love Muriel.'

This poignant photograph of six Suffolk lads posing among the ruins of Arras, a French town that had been destroyed by shellfire, was taken in the autumn of 1916. Chris Winyard, Ted Upcraft, Sid Barnes, Wally Spence, and Tommy Doy were from Southwold, and Corporal Shaw hailed from Great Yarmouth. Tommy Doy won a Military Medal for storming a German machine-gun nest and all six survived the war. But by the end of 1916 twenty-three Southwold servicemen had been killed in action.

News of the fighting in France appeared in newspapers sold by Chapman's, the tobacconist and newsagent, but it was also received in telegrams which were displayed in the shop windows. Southwold was a story itself when a flotilla of German destroyers appeared off the town on the night of 15 January 1917, and fired ninety-two shells into it. Only the police station and two houses were hit, and no-one was killed or injured.

Southwold had an uncomfortable night in April 1915 when the weird burr of a German Zeppelin was heard over the town. It went on to drop several incendiary bombs on Henham Park, and two at Reydon. Southwold railway station was apparently a target and one bomb fell in an empty coal truck, making a hole in the bottom.

The war memorial near the church gate on St Bartholomew Green was dedicated at a moving ceremony in July 1921. It has the names of fifty-one men and one woman who were killed during the First World War. The names of twenty servicemen who died in action during the Second World War and thirteen civilians killed by bombing were added.

A victory dinner hosted by the Mayor, Mr Charles Fowler, was held in January 1920 when all servicemen who had taken part in the war had been demobilised and had returned to the town. The dinner was held in the Constitutional Hall on South Green, which was to be totally destroyed by a 1,000 lb bomb in November 1940.

The highlight of Southwold's year was, and still is to some extent, the Trinity Fair. Under the terms of a charter granted by King Henry VII in 1489 the town is entitled to hold a fair on three days succeeding Trinity Sunday. It gets under way with the town clerk reading an ancient proclamation at three different spots. This photograph was taken on Trinity Monday 1912, when a large crowd gathered to hear the proclamation. There is a policeman on the right of the picture to maintain public order.

There were few trees in Southwold before 1900. Conventional wisdom was that trees did not do well by the sea, so why plant them? But 1908 saw a tree planting festival on St Edmund's Green opposite the hospital, involving the Mayor Mr E.W. Moore and other dignitaries. This evolved into a regular annual Arbor Day ceremony involving schoolchildren and other groups.

Being mobbed by this crowd on Southwold beach in 1938 is King George VI who had a fear of public occasions amounting to a phobia. As the Duke of York he had taken part in the pre-war annual Camp on The Common. Although he had become King he still came to Southwold to attend the Camp.

King George VI was crowned in Westminster Abbey, and it became another special Southwold occasion. The High Street was ablaze with flags and bunting, and there were events on The Common including a royal pageant.

Beating the Bounds may or may not be an ancient Roman ceremony but it has been taking place from time to time in Southwold for more than 100 years. This photograph dates from 1911 when the rite was performed to mark King George V's coronation. The Mayor and other local dignitaries accompanied by the Town Band walked the boundaries of the town, nearly 5 miles, with long thin sticks. In former times these would be used to beat or bump small boys accompanying the party. The ceremony ended at the Harbour Inn, Blackshore, where the King was toasted with ale.

The Mortlock family, 1940. This family portrait with the four brothers Frank, Harry, Ronnie and Harold, and Ivy, Edie, Ethel and grandmother Edith, not forgetting Panda the labrador, was the last time the family could all get together until 1946 when the war had ended.

At the start of the Second World War several dozen children were evacuated from London to Southwold. But after the evacuation of Dunkirk in 1940 Southwold became part of the front line. Now the children became evacuees themselves. The Junior School was closed and forty children with two teachers, Miss Walters and Miss Palin, and the headmistress, Miss Brooks, were evacuated to Worksop in Nottinghamshire. The school reopened on 3 September 1946.

A lone German bomber dived out of the cloud one morning in February 1943 and dropped one 1,000 lb bomb which scored a direct hit on a house in Pier Avenue. Another twenty houses were damaged but no-one was killed.

In March 1941 Gun Hill Fort was established in the front garden of Marine Villa. This was a nice touch of historical continuity as it was less than 50 yards from where the six-gun battery had been, before being buried to avoid giving the Germans any excuse to shell or bomb the town. Two elderly 6-inch guns were installed facing slightly south-west to cover Sole Bay, and a battery observation post was set up in a nearby house. It is not known whether the guns were ever fired in anger before being taken away for scrap in November 1945. The spot has reverted to being a front garden overlooking the promenade.

A peace bonfire on The Common and street parties for children were among the ways the town marked the end of the Second World War in 1945. This party was held in Cautley Road outside the headquarters of the Girl Guides. Soon barbed wire defences along the promenade were removed and the beaches were cleared of mines. The remains of the old bathing machines placed on The Common to hinder German aircraft wanting to land were taken away and dumped. Southwold had survived 119 high-explosive bombs, 2,689 incendiaries, two parachute mines and a single flying bomb. Thirteen civilians were killed and forty-nine injured. More than 2,000 properties were damaged.

HMS *Sole Bay*, the town's adopted destroyer, never lost an opportunity to maintain links with Southwold. In 1951 it berthed in Sole Bay, and local schoolchildren were invited aboard for a party and a tour of the warship.

In 1958 the destroyer took part in a major military exercise, 'Operation Para Handy', when the Ministry of Defence used South Beach as a strip of desert coastline of an imaginary British protectorate. A thousand men were involved, and during the exercise troops stormed ashore from landing craft and quickly 'occupied' Ferry Road to the astonishment of watching holidaymakers.

A special Southwold occasion is the night the town switches on its Christmas lights. Several thousand people flock to the Market Square to see the arrival of Father Christmas, listen to bands and the choir, join in the carols and cheer the fireworks. In 1953 a huge wooden chalet, complete with a man-sized Father Christmas and sleigh, was built in the Market Square, and there was an event every night right up to Christmas.

CHAPTER SEVEN

WORK

The Centre Cliff Hotel advertised itself in 1900 as being 'direct from Liverpool Street Station, London'. A charming hotel belonging to Adnams, it was beautifully positioned above Kilcock Cliff, and a new wing was built in 1899 giving an additional thirty bedrooms. The staff posed for this photograph in 1905, when the manager was Mrs Amelia Downer and the horse-drawn bus met every train and boat. Like the Grand Hotel it was used for billeting troops during the Second World War, suffered damage and was turned into houses and flats.

Ale was the staple drink of England for centuries, and in Southwold taverns brewing their own ale and one-roomed beer houses abounded. In 1872 George and Ernest Adnams arrived to put their stamp on the town. They took over the Sole Bay Brewery, shown in this photograph of the late 1860s, which had roots going back to 1345. A sizeable estate of twenty pubs was created and the brewery was enlarged and rebuilt. Effectively this was the beginning of the Adnams empire. Nowadays it is the largest single employer in Southwold, the heartbeat of a living working town.

Adnams cautiously expanded during the 1920s by taking over breweries in Orford and Aldeburgh, which brought new outlets and sold more pints. The workforce was increased and now the brewery could field a tug-o-war team. The 1923 team is shown here. Back row, left to right: A. Collins, Arthur Upcraft, Mr Palmer, the brewer, G. Clow and 'Duke' Osborne. Front row: George 'Clump' Sagin, 'Shorty' Martin, Tom Fletcher and his son, Harry Button. The brewery cat has also got into the picture.

In 1914 Adnams bought its first mechanical vehicle, a Foden steamer and trailer. The driver was George Wilding and the steersman George Sagin, and there were some accidents as they drove the vehicle through Suffolk lanes. Percheron horses, a truly majestic sight, still pull Adnams drays around the town delivering beer.

Adnams Tally Ho was first brewed in 1880 as this early marketing photograph shows. In 1904 it was 2s per gallon. It is still sold today in bottles as a classic barley wine, a heart-warming Christmas ale.

The elegant Swan Hotel pleasantly dominating the Market Place is the quintessence of all that is gracefully Georgian in Southwold. First licensed in 1763, it is the town's principal hotel. This photograph was taken in 1897 when it described itself as a family and commercial hotel and posting house with good coffee rooms, billiards and bath rooms, liberal table, and carriages for hire. A few years later it was to face competition from two other hotels, the Grand and the Marlborough, which was destroyed during a bombing raid in 1943.

This evocative picture was taken in Field Style Road in 1899. B. Goldsmith is holding the horse's head and Throoker Palmer is on the right. Holding the reins in the delivery cart is Jack Fryett, a pork butcher trading from 32 East Street, and his son.

Another popular local trader was Frederick Eastaugh, the baker and confectioner of 64 High Street.

Denny and Son, Market Place, 1901. Known as the Harrods of Southwold, the shop begun trading in Lorne Road before moving to the Market Place in 1895 as gentlemen's outfitters. It has had many distinguished customers such as Sir Alfred Munnings, the artist, Benjamin Britten, the composer who lived at Aldeburgh, and Eric Blair, better known as George Orwell. Orwell's parents came to live in Southwold in 1933 and he often visited them. With his socialist views and his middle-class guilt Orwell was prone to dislike Southwold, with its Tory Council and many retired gentlefolk, but he continued to have his suits made by Denny's after he left.

Francis 'Porky' Goffin outside his shop at 21 High Street, with the White Horse, a beer house, next door, 1901. He ran the shop as a pork butcher until the early 1920s when he switched to selling sweets, including a popular gobstopper. The shop reverted to being a butcher's when it was taken over by the Lowestoft Co-operative Society. In the photograph below the turkeys are strung up for Christmas 1928 and some are already labelled. Today the shop would be in trouble with the local health and safety officials. The premises became an antique shop and finally a private house.

Beginning with four workers making hosiery in 1909, the Homeknit company expanded to employ more than 100 people making jumpers, suits and other knitted garments of high quality which were sold to large London stores. The company closed in 1960 and a new telephone exchange was built on the site at the corner of Pier Avenue. This float took part in events to mark the Silver Jubilee of King George V and Queen Mary in 1935.

The town's last flour mill was not a windmill but a well-built brick factory at North Green with good stabling and the Marquis of Lorne inn as a neighbour. It closed in 1918 to become a factory employing forty people making mattresses, pillows and divans for Slumberland, who were to shut it down in 1976. The building was converted to flats.

The King's Head was the residence of James Magg, the Southwold diarist, teacher and auctioneer, but when this photograph was taken in the 1880s it was well established as a pub. Above the saloon door is an advertisement for the *Daily Telegraph*, which sold for 1*d*.

CHAPTER EIGHT

GETTING THERE

*To great rejoicing by the local population the Southwold Railway was opened on 24 September 1879, linking
the town with Halesworth and thus connecting with the main line from London. It was one of the few narrow
gauge branch lines England has ever had and it brought about more change to the town than any other event
in its history. For the next 50 years four 'Thomas the Tank' engines pulled clanking maroon carriages of
holidaymakers and creaking trucks with freight to Southwold, and took fish from the town and milk from
Blythburgh to markets in London.*

Southwold railway station, *c.* 1900. In this charming photograph the Railway Children, about to leave town, are seen off by a passing dog. There is a magnificent high-wheeled perambulator and everyone is wearing something on their heads, for the railway station was one of the important places where it was imperative to be properly dressed. This photograph appears by kind permission of the Southwold Railway Society, formed to promote the memory of the old railway.

The bridge over the River Blyth, 1879. Built for the railway, the swing bridge had a span of 146 ft, and was locked into position by a heavy key carried on the engines. It was rarely opened but was considered to be an elegant feature especially at high tide. During the Second World War it was blown up by the army in the interests of national security.

The interior of a third-class carriage, 1908. Passengers sat on wooden seats covered by strips of stair carpet, and a return ticket to Halesworth cost 1s. First-class passengers had blue cushions and they paid double. The coaches were lit by oil lamps and in the winter straw covered the floor, while first-class passengers had hot water foot warmers.

There were no ticket barriers or fencing at the station and the portmanteaux, hatboxes and trunks would be carried by porters to W. Doy's waiting carts, or to buses despatched by hotels. The 3 ft wide track ran for nearly 9 miles along a scenic route to Halesworth and took about thirty-five minutes. It had a speed restriction of 16 mph imposed by the Board of Trade, and the story is told of how an old lady was walking alongside the line when a train slowly approached from behind. The driver pulled up and said: 'Would yar like a lift, missis?' To which she replied: 'No thanks, I'm in a hurry.'

Walberswick was the first stop from Southwold, and this photograph was taken in 1902 after a telephone system was installed. From here the little train chugged across a fine heath moorland, beneath tall pines where herons nest to this day, and skirted the wide estuary flats leading to Blythburgh. Some sections of the track have become popular footpaths, while the rest have reverted to nature or been taken by adjacent landowners.

A holiday train has arrived and there is a traffic jam involving carriages and carts. In the foreground are two gypsies from neighbouring Wenhaston selling lace and pegs and looking for customers. Note the simple advertising of about 1910.

The last passenger train from Southwold puffed out of the station at 5.23 p.m. on 11 April 1929 with a wreath placed on the engine. Some of the passengers had travelled on the first journey fifty years earlier. The railway had peaked in 1912, when more than 100,000 passengers were using the line every year and some 13,000 tons of freight was being moved. But motor buses had been licensed by the Southwold Corporation to pick up fares in the town and were operating to the big towns such as Lowestoft, and the day of the motor car had arrived. It was the end of the line for the Southwold Railway.

A motor omnibus service operated between Southwold and Lowestoft from July 1904 to January 1913. The three buses on the route belonged to the Great Eastern Railway. This photograph is of a 24 hp Thornycroft bus of 1907.

There is no room on the top of this bus leaving Southwold for Lowestoft. This postcard was sent from Southwold in 1907 with a message on the back: 'Dear Cookie, The gingerbread proved most acceptable and sustaining. I ate it on the bus top when I was beginning to feel cold and rather miserable and I thank you again for it. Love Ezzie.'

This photograph shows passengers gathering in the High Street on 25 March 1929 for seats on the first motor coach to travel from Southwold to London. Buses leave from Southwold at nearly the same spot today.

This Benz Dogcart was the first motor car to be seen in Southwold and caused great excitement when it drove up the High Street in 1904. It is believed that the gentleman with the top hat who is sitting next to his chauffeur is the Earl of Stradbroke.

This motor car was parked outside Goddard's, the town's cycle dealer and repairer, in 1908. It is a 10/12 hp Darracq. Its occupants are unknown, but Mr Goddard is standing outside his shop with the 'cycles built' sign above his head.

The chain ferry across the River Blyth operated from 1885 to 1942 and took passengers and carts, and later motor cars. It worked by hand crank and chains until converted to steam power in 1899. The ferry was effectively abandoned following the rebuilding of Southwold harbour in 1937. The bell-shaped mouth funnelled waves up the harbour making the river too rough for it to operate.

The ferry linking Southwold to Walberswick dates from 1236 when the Lady of the Manor of Blythburgh and Walberswick was charged to keep a ferry boat on her side of the river. Before, and after, the chain ferry the crossing was made by rowing boat. This exquisite picture dates from the 1880s when George Todd was the ferryman. (Southwold Museum)

Todd was the last ferryman before the chain ferry took over the role. But during the Second World War the ferry was restarted to take soldiers based in Walberswick across the river to the cinema. After the war the Cross family carried on ferrying, and now, in the summer, locals and holidaymakers can be rowed across the Blyth.

King George VI came to Southwold to attend his much-loved summer camp for the last time in 1938. He was rowed ashore from the royal yacht, the *Victoria and Albert III*, by two local fishermen, Prim Deal and Dykes Stannard.

The Royal Sussex Cyclists were stationed in Southwold for eleven months during the First World War. They left as they arrived, on their bicycles.

The pier was built in 1900 to take Belle steamers which ran for many years between London and Great Yarmouth. From the end of June to the middle of September the steamer left London Bridge at 8.55 in the morning and stopped at the pier, returning in the evening. In 1919 return tickets cost 7s 6d in the fore cabin, and 10s for a place in the saloon. The service ended in 1928 and six years later the head of the pier was washed away. More damage was done to it during the Second World War, and gales finished off the rest of the pier in 1979.

ACKNOWLEDGEMENTS

This book began as a personal millennium project but it would not have been possible without the co-operation and enthusiasm of a great many Southwold people. Their readiness to share their knowledge such as identifying faces, places and occasions, and their willingness to share their photographs and postcards with a wider audience has been greatly appreciated, and a delight.

I am especially indebted to: John Purdy, David Lee, Ronnie Waters, Lennie Doy, John Burrage, George Bumstead, Frank Mortlock, Leslie Barber, Reg Block, Bernard Segrave Daly, Denis Stannard, John Uden, Peter Webb, Peter Mace, John Pigneguy, David Hoon, Dutta Doy, John Bennett, Dudley Clarke, Nick Walmsley, Stephen Wolfenden, Margaret Storer, Nancy Pelling, Shirley Cordeaux, Lyn Knights, Molly Robinson, Sue Doy, Beattie King, Ros Macdermott, Alice Denny, Barbara Davis, Joyce Davis, Joan Jarvis, Rachael Lawrence, Mary Smith, Sheena Chisnell, Catherine Horwood, Mary Trumpess, the Committee of St Barnabas, Southwold Red Cross, the Lowestoft Record Office, the Suffolk Record Office, and Richard Wells of Wells Photo and Audio Ltd, Southwold.

Finally I would also like to thank Alicia Jenkins, daughter of Frederick Jenkins, for loaning me photographs and making available details of her father's life and work. Devotees of Southwold might like to know that some of the photographs used in this book have appeared in four books published by the family and on sale in Southwold. They are: *A Visit to Southwold, Reminiscences of Southwold during the two World Wars, A Photographic Collection of Bygones and Local Characters of Southwold* and *Barrett Jenkins' Southwold 1904–1992.*

BRITAIN IN OLD PHOTOGRAPHS

SUTTON'S PHOTOGRAPHIC HISTORY OF TRANSPORT

To order any of these titles please telephone our distributor, Littlehampton Book Services on 01903 828800
For a catalogue of these and our other titles please ring Emma Leitch on 01453 731114